Seward's Other Folly:
America's First Encrypted Cable

On the early morning of 26 November 1866, a secret encrypted cable from Secretary of State William Seward began arriving in the Paris telegraph office. The dispatch's last installment was completed at 4:30 the following afternoon. "I immediately discerned," wrote American minister to France John Bigelow, "that it was written more for the edification of Congress than for mine, for Mr. Seward knew full well at the moment of writing it that the Emperor [of France] and his Cabinet were all more anxious than any citizen of the United States to hasten the recall of their troops from Mexico, and that they were doing everything that was possible to that end."[1] News and rumors about the lengthy encoded telegram spread rapidly through the French governmental departments and the diplomatic corps: legation representatives flooded Bigelow's office with inquiries. Bigelow maintained a determined silence. The first steamer from New York to arrive in France after the dispatch was written brought a reprint of the confidential cable in the pages of the *New York Herald*. A confident Bigelow smiled: the reprint "confirmed my first impression that it was written for Congress rather than for the Tuileries."[2]

> 1436, one hundred nine, 109, arrow, twelve sixty-four, 1264, fourteen hundred one, 1401, fifteen forty-four, 1544, three sixty, 360, two hundred eight, 208, eleven hundred eight, 1108, five twenty, 520, five sixty-nine, 569, ten sixty-eight, 1068, six fifty-three, 653, six sixty-eight, 668, fourteen forty, 1440, fourteen thirty-six, 1436, three sixty-six, 366, four seventy-nine, 479, seventy, 70, five sixty-nine, 569, eight forty-six, 846, four ninety-one, 491, cross, eleven seventy-three, 1173, thirteen eighty-five, 1385, seventy-eight, 78, ten forty-seven, 1047, nine hundred eight, 908, ten forty-seven, 1047, three sixty, 360, twelve fifty-nine, 1259, fifteen

Extract from Seward dispatch to Bigelow

This strange episode in American foreign relations commenced a fascinating chapter in American cryptologic history. Moreover, the event shaped American State Department codebooks for the next two generations and also precipitated a costly lawsuit against the United States government.

Several months earlier Bigelow wrote William Seward about the receipt of an inaugural dispatch from the Atlantic cable entrepreneur, Cyrus Field, who transmitted a special message from Newfoundland to Paris: "The Atlantic cable is successfully laid: may it prove a blessing to all mankind."[3] Bigelow also joined in singing the chorus of congratulations and praised what he termed the "umbilical cord with which the old world is reunited to its transatlantic offspring."

Cyrus Field

Politically astute and with an acute awareness of European government communications security practices because of his European travels, Bigelow, who became consul-general in Paris in 1861 and minister in 1865, recognized the new challenges for communications security that accompanied the new Atlantic cable. He strongly advised Seward to develop a new cipher for the exclusive use of the State Department so that Seward could communicate secretly with his diplomatic officers; even better, he suggested a different cipher for each of the legations. He warned Seward, "It is not likely that it would suit the purposes of the Government to have its telegrams for this Legation read first by the French authorities, and yet you are well aware that nothing goes over a French telegraph wire, that is not transmitted to the Ministry of the Interior."[4]

More worrisome to Bigelow was his belief that the State Department code was no longer secret, for he believed copies of it were taken from the State Department archives by the "traitors to the Government under Mr. Buchanan's administration," and the principal European governments now had the key. In conclusion, Bigelow added, the department should take steps to "clothe its communications with that privacy without which, oftentimes, they would become valueless."[5]

Seward's naive reply to Bigelow's dispatch dismissed the conjecture that traitors took copies of the code by stating that the code sheets were always in the custody of the department's loyal chief clerk or clerk in charge of the French and other missions.

Moreover, if a person were to make a copy, it would take at least two long working days if he had the necessary blank forms, and at least a week without the forms. Then Seward, continuing to write as a person who had never used the code, noted that a variation of a single figure or letter would spoil the whole code. And he added an astonishing statement: the Department code, in service for at least half a century, was believed to be the "most inscrutable ever invented."[6] Seward wrote that he, together with earlier secretaries of state, held this opinion, and therefore the Department rejected the offer of five or six new ciphers each year. Apparently, Secretary Seward's management skills did not include an understanding of communications security,

William H. Seward

especially in a European atmosphere.[7] Nor did he understand the administration of cable communications when codes or ciphers were involved. Bigelow thought Seward too talented and ambitious to be satisfied with being merely a political swashbuckler; rather the secretary tried to rank with the leaders of men. However, "his wings, like those of the ostrich, though they served him to run with greater speed, could not lift him entirely from the ground . . . . If he did not march as fast as some, he always kept ahead of his troops, but never so far that they could not hear his word of command."[8]

On 29 August 1866, a gala dinner honoring President Andrew Johnson was held in New York City. At the end of the evening, Mr. Wilson G. Hunt, one of the directors of the New York, Newfoundland, and London Telegraph Company, approached Secretary Seward and asked him why the federal government did not use the new Atlantic cable, which had just been completed on July 28. It was a question that would eventually lead to a $32,000 claim against the United States State Department. Replying to Hunt, Seward said that the tariff was too costly, that "the Government of the United States was not rich enough to use the Telegraph."[9] Seward's judgment, though exaggerated, was somewhat accurate because the provisional tariff rates, adopted 1 July 1865, were very expensive: cable charges between America and Great Britain were $100 or 20 pounds sterling for messages of twenty words or less, including address, date and signature: every additional word, not exceeding five letters, cost 20 shillings per word. Between America and Continental Europe, charges were 21 pounds for twenty words. Code or cipher messages were charged double.[10] All messages, according to the tariff, had to be paid in gold before transmission.[11]

Seward explained to Hunt that "the government was too poor to use the cable, because the charges for its use, according to a tariff which was reported, were too high, and practically oppressive and extortionate."[12]   Seward alarmed Hunt when he declared, "under that tariff, the Atlantic cable would, as a medium of communication between governments in Europe and America, be a failure; that the United States government would not use it, and I had learned from foreign ministers residing in Washington that they could not use it."[13] Indeed, Seward explained, he had earlier prepared a message to send to one of the American ministers abroad, and referred it to the telegraph company for transmission; however, on learning the estimated charges (Hunt believed Seward mentioned the cost at about $680), he cancelled the request and sent the dispatch by mail.[14]

In addition, Seward said, the immense Civil War debt facing the United States required economy and frugality. He was acutely aware that the federal government had spent over three billion dollars during the four years of conflict; moreover, the federal debt equalled almost one half of the gross national product. Government leaders faced the largest debt the United States had ever experienced: the interest alone surpassed the federal debt before 1861.[15] In fact, Seward's overseas budget had been recently reduced from $140,000 for the fiscal year ending June 1866 to $115,000 for 1867. The State Department, Seward added, would lose public confidence if it incurred the great expense of telegraphic communication under the existing tariff. Moreover, Seward recognized that a code or cipher must be employed for telegraphic communication in order to maintain corifidentiality; and using the U.S. "cipher code" for a cable at the time "increased the number of words about five times, and the expense of transmission ten times."[16] Erroneously, Seward believed the State Department code then current was the only one used since the federal government had been organized.

An anxious Hunt told Seward that the telegraph tariff had been adopted on the grounds of the cable's novelty, and also it resulted from managerial inexperience with setting rates. He urged Seward to convey the State Department's objections in a written communication to the company proprietors. Seward either promised or indicated he might do so, perhaps after further reflection and consultation with the president.[17]

Seward said he believed it was at this time that Hunt asked what rates the government paid the domestic telegraph company. Seward replied that the War Department "conducts that business exclusively" under regulations made by the War Department, that the "war telegraph was a war instrument, and as I understood it, we fixed our own prices and paid what we pleased."[18] However, Seward's understanding was mistaken, for the government paid regular rates on Western Union lines. According to Seward, Hunt asked whether Seward would use the Atlantic cable telegraph by way of trial in the same way as the domestic telegraph adaptation until some definite arrangement could be made satisfactory to all. Seward promised to use the cable when a proper occasion arose, and they both agreed that the government would do what was just, and he hoped the telegraph proprietors would be equally reasonable.

According to Seward's account, Hunt and he had the understanding that Seward could pay what he thought proper for the trial use of the cable, and, moreover, that Seward should either send the dispatch to Hunt's care or advise him that the cable had been given to the agent so that the trial message would not be sent under the regular tariff, but subject to the special trial arrangement. A bystander later recalled Seward's emphasis upon economy but when questioned further had no recollection of the trial message option. Nor did Hunt, in his later deposition, recall any special trial message arrangement.[19]

The after-dinner conversation between Hunt and Seward ended with Hunt's belief he would soon receive a written message from Seward with a request for lower rates. Seward, in turn, said he believed he could send a trial message as an experiment for lowering rates. The seeds of confusion, planted during this brief conversation, would grow when Seward failed to send the written communication to the company's proprietors.

Seward also had allies in his complaints about the exorbitant cable tariffs. An editorial in *The New York Times* praised the ingenuity that provided telegraphic communication between the two continents, an "achievement much more grand than the 'Hanging Gardens of Babylon' or any other one of the wonders of the Old World."[20] However, the *Times* added that this monopoly should not "bleed the people." This newspaper and other large east coast publications were eager to lower their costs for the cables sent to them by foreign correspondents. Prices, the editor wrote, must be lowered: $5 in gold per five-letter word was too expensive. And with pleasure, the *Times* reported six weeks later on a letter from Cyrus W. Field that on and after 1 November 1866, Atlantic cable rates would be reduced fifty percent.[21] Negotiations between the New York, Newfoundland, and London Telegraph Company and the Anglo-American Telegraph Company resulted in the lowered tariff: messages of twenty words for $50 to Great Britain, and $51.25 to Paris. Code and cipher messages would still be charged double.[22]

Wilson Hunt sent Seward a listing of the new prices. Ten days after the new tariff went into effect and to the delight of the cable company, Seward sent, in plain text, the very first State Department cable via the Western Union Telegraph Company. It was a brief dispatch to John Bigelow, the American minister to France, simply telling him that his successor, General John A. Dix, would embark on the *Fulton* on 24 November.[23] Although cable company rules required prepayment for all messages, the State Department did not pay the charges of $60.37 for twenty-three words until the following May.[24] Cable company directors now hoped the federal government would send frequent communications via the Atlantic cable.

On 15 November 1866, in New York City's Metropolitan Hotel banquet hall, 300 invited merchants, bankers, and other distinguished guests attended a banquet honoring Cyrus W. Field for his outstanding work in the thirteen-year project for the laying of the Atlantic cable.

In his remarks to the banquet guests, Field recounted the tremendous difficulties over the previous thirteen years, especially for financing and constructing the complicated project that consisted of four telegraph lines: London to Valentia, Ireland; Valentia to Heart's Content, Newfoundland; Heart's Content to Port Hood, Nova Scotia; and Port Hood to New York City. He gave special gratitude to British financiers for their enormous support over the years even though over $1 million had been spent by New York investors for the western terminus of the cable before a penny had been spent in England for the project. He also emphasized his hope that it would take no longer than twenty minutes for messages to reach New York from London: indeed, he thought a message from Wall Street to the Royal Exchange in London could be answered and returned to New York in an hour, even by allowing ten minutes on each side for a boy to carry the dispatch from the telegraph office to the business office.

Sensitive to the press and private complaints about the costly, indeed oppressive, tariffs, Field explained that the investment totaled $12 million. The managers initially were worried that the cable might again break; in fact, Field reported, some prophets predicted it might last only one month. And now the company had two cables instead of only one, and a third distinct line was planned. Experience had shown that instead of five words a minute, operators could send fifteen. Thus, after only three months of operations the tariff was reduced by just one half, and he hoped it would soon be brought down to one quarter.

Wilson Hunt's earlier request to Seward for greater government use of the cable would be answered a week after the New York banquet in honor of Field. Threatening events in Mexico, where French troops supported a European emperor, forced Seward to consider sending a secret encrypted warning to the French emperor, Napoleon III. The continuing revolution and warfare in Mexico had troubled the secretary all during the American Civil War. He feared this new expansion of a French empire in America. And with the war's conclusion, the situation along America's southern border now became a major foreign policy problem confronting Seward.[25]

Seward believed it was necessary to send a dispatch to his minister in France, John Bigelow, encoded because his highly confidential message would pass through American and foreign telegrapher hands. However, encoded American diplomatic dispatches had become a distinct rarity in the years after 1848, the end of the War with Mexico.

During the American Civil War, French armed forces, under orders of Napoleon III, captured Mexico City and in 1864 arranged for Archduke Ferdinand Maximilian of Austria to take over the Mexican throne. A shrewd Secretary of State William Seward, anxious about potential French support for the Southern armies if he complained too vigorously about French intervention in Mexico, patiently waited until Southern military forces no longer threatened the Union.

In the months immediately after the South's surrender at Appomattox, the apprehensive Seward pressured Napoleon III to withdraw his military forces in Mexico, then numbering 28,000 men. According to Seward, this withdrawal would enable the Mexican people to choose between Maximilian as emperor and Juarez as president.[26] In January 1866, the French emperor ordered his military staff in Mexico, headed by Marshal Francois Achille Bazaine, to prepare for evacuation from Mexico. By April, the emperor agreed that 28,000 French troops would leave in three stages: November 1866, and March and November 1867.[27] In late May, Bigelow was told the French troops would be withdrawn, probably sooner than the scheduled time.[28] In June, Maximilian received word from Napoleon III that the French army was being sent home. In late August, press accounts stated that Napoleon had been visited by the Empress Carlotta, Maximilian's wife, recently arrived from Mexico. She requested an extension of the time for the departure of the French troops from Mexico, and Napoleon granted her wish.[29]

A "back channel" to Seward was opened by the French government when it sent a French agent, John D'Oyley Evans, from Paris with an informal and verbal message from the French foreign minister, Drouyn de Lhuys, and Emperor Napoleon. Calling at the State Department on 17 September 1866, Evans learned that Seward was confined to his room by a severe illness. He informed Frederick W. Seward, the assistant secretary, that the French government would "faithfully and fairly adhere to the very letter of the understanding between France and the U.S. in regard to the evacuation of Mexico."[30]

Press accounts in France and Mexico about the emperor's disposition to change the evacuation schedule, complained Secretary Seward on 8 October, had produced a large popular mistrust of the emperor's sincerity. He emphasized that the State Department continued to insist upon the fulfillment of the letter and spirit of the evacuation of the French forces in Mexico. Clearly, Secretary Seward exhibited nervousness about the French maneuvers, whether reported in the press, or by confidential messengers.[31] And Seward, reading the American newspapers, witnessed the unusual interest of editors in the American foreign policy crisis precipitated by France. Also, because the American diplomatic dispatches were promptly published in the daily press, it seemed American diplomacy was being conducted in the newspapers.

John Bigelow sent an alarming dispatch to Seward, dated 8 November 1866, and explained that the French ruler had decided to delay withdrawal of any troops until spring: at that time he would remove all his troops, but none before that time.[32] Recent successes of Mexican troops, reinforced by American volunteers, required the continued presence of all the French forces. Moreover, the emperor assured Bigelow that he had telegraphed the message to delay troop removal to Bazaine in plain text, not cipher, in order to forestall any rumors about new secret French designs in Mexico. When Bigelow protested that the French government may not have notified President Andrew Johnson of this dangerous change in plans, Napoleon replied that the existence of the new Atlantic cable lessened the threat of communications misunderstandings.[33] Finally, Napoleon III related that he had advised Maximilian to abdicate.[34]

Seward read Bigelow's dispatch with anger and frustration. In addition, the Republican administration had just witnessed defeat in the recent congressional elections. Some of the opponents were planning to attack President Johnson in the Congress. A forceful cable to France might overcome the opposition, or at least lessen its criticism. And promptly releasing the dispatch to the newspapers would demonstrate the administration's resolve.[35]

Seward's stern reply of 23 November (transmitted 24 November), encoded in the Monroe code first used in 1803, was completed a day after receiving Bigelow's dispatch, and the response was scheduled for transmission on the transatlantic cable: Seward thought in accord with the trial cost basis reached with Hunt at the previous August dinner in New York City.[36] Seward said that he had written his message with the expectation that Bigelow would read the dispatch to the emperor. Because of this, no word was left out for reasons of economy. Also, before transmitting, Seward submitted the message to President Johnson and the cabinet, which met in an unusual session the afternoon of the 23d, and they approved Seward's dispatch without amendment or change.[37] One cabinet member commented on the potentially costly expense of sending the cable; however, Seward explained to the president and the cabinet that he had made an arrangement with Mr. Hunt whereby he could set the price for any dispatch he chose to send. Also, Seward testified later, he had directed one of his subordinates to inform Mr. Hunt of the dispatch at the time of the transmission: he had no recollection whether this was done or not.[38] Actually, someone had alerted Hunt to the existence of the cable, and Hunt telegraphed Seward on Sunday, 25 November, that the dispatch had been sent on to Paris on the previous night.[39]

The encoded Seward dispatch, termed a "pungent remonstrance to the French government" by *The New York Herald*, was given at 6 P.M. on 23 November to the manager of the War Department telegraph office, Charles A. Tinker , for transmission.[40] Tinker recalled the original dispatch was written only in figures and that cable office rules required him to spell out the figures in letters and transmit the letters and figures. He immediately sent for another operator to make a copy of the dispatch so that he might return the original to the State Department and still retain one for his files. Tinker began to transmit the dispatch by 6:15, and it was repeated back to his office so that by 12:15 A.M. the process was finished. It was the longest cable dispatch – 3,722 words – he had ever sent.

The Seward historic cryptographic document became the first encoded American diplomatic dispatch to use the new Atlantic cable. A State Department clerk, John H. Haswell, who prepared the cable, recalled much later: "The first cablegram [actually it was the second] sent by the Department was an important one addressed to our minister at Paris. It caused the French to leave Mexico. I was directed by the Secretary to send it in cipher, using the Department's code, which had been in vogue since colonial times but seldom used." Despite its age, Haswell wrote, "It was a good one, but entirely unsuited for telegraphic communication. Its cumbersome character, and what was of even more importance, the very great expense entailed by its use impressed me, and turned my attention to an arrangement for cipher communication by telegraph."[41]

Seward's arguments in the cable, formulated like a lawyer's brief, stressed that the emperor had failed to confer with or notify President Johnson regarding modification of the earlier troop withdrawal schedule. Moreover, the evacuation promised for the spring offered no guarantee of fulfillment; and the change in the timetable interfered with ongoing extraordinary efforts of the United States to cooperate with Mexico for pacifying and restoring proper constitutional authority in the southern republic. Seward concluded with the expectation that the emperor would telegraph or mail a satisfactory resolution in reply to this dispatch; moreover, he wrote that President Johnson believed the French expeditionary forces would be completely removed within the eighteen months originally stipulated.[42]

The New York Herald featured the French evacuation story on 29 November with a brief article under the heading, "What is the Meaning of that Long Dispatch?" This account reported a telegram had just been received from London that revealed Bigelow had received a long dispatch and that it was related to "some new hitch in the Mexican difficulty." Additional reports in that newspaper on 1 and 2 December repeated the story that the telegraph focused on the French troops in Mexico; and on 7 December, the *Herald* described Seward's testimony before the Senate Committee on Foreign Relations. Moreover, Seward provided the full plain text of his secret dispatch. For more than six decades, the Monroe code had provided a modest degree of protection; however, Seward's maneuvers with the committee, and possibly the *Herald*, greatly lessened communications security and the value of the code.

The *Herald* also applauded the Seward dispatch with an editorial that stated, "It is an improvement upon all his preceding correspondence on this subject since the close of the rebellion. . . . there is something of credit due even to Mr. Seward, for the patience, the diligence, and the tenacity with which he had held to his text, until we may say he has literally scolded Napoleon out of Mexico."[43]

The Seward encrypted cable began as follows:

Washington,
November twenty-third, eighteen sixty-six

John Bigelow, Esquire,
United States Minister, Paris.

Sir. – Your dispatch, number three eighty-four, 384, in regard to six twenty-eight, 628, six fifty-one, 651, fourteen hundred four;   fifteen fifty-one, 1551, is received . . . .[44]

Bigelow did not read the dispatch to the emperor; rather, his calm response to the lengthy cable told of his note of inquiry to the French minister of foreign affairs, who was out of the city. Receiving no answer, Bigelow pressed the issue further with still another inquiry requesting an explanation of the emperor's motives for deferring the partial evacuation of the troops. In an interview on 30 November, the minister of state and government's spokesman in the legislature, M. Eugene Rouher, told Bigelow the transport vessels were ready and waiting at Vera Cruz and that commanders expected to have the force returned to France by March, at the latest. [45] Bigelow also used the cable to reply in code to Seward that there would be collective repatriation in March and that the French government desired friendly relations with the United States. The minister also informed Seward that his reply from Paris cost over 9,160 francs ($1,833).[46]

Seward's confidential dispatch to Bigelow contained more than thirty-five transmission errors; some phrases were mistakenly repeated twice in the cablegram. Many of these errors occurred during the rewrite process when the cable clerk substituted words for the numbers; thus, for example, "1424" was incorrectly sent as "fourteen twenty six." Seward's original plaintext message of 780 words, when encoded, became 1,237 number groups with 88 additional code symbols, such as a cross and an arrow, spelled out. These groups and symbols plus the address were rendered into 3,722 words for transmission.[47]

During December, Charles A. Keefer, a cipher clerk for General Philip Sheridan in New Orleans, would provide invaluable information regarding the French withdrawal from Mexico. This young man was one of twenty Union operators who came to the United States from Canada and the other northern provinces.[48] Almost certainly, Keefer was the first in the United States service to use communications intelligence in peacetime. In mid-December, he wrote to General Ulysses S. Grant that he had happened to be in the New Orleans telegraph office on 9 December when a message from Napoleon to General Castelnau in Mexico was being transmitted via the French consulate in New Orleans. He copied the message, translated it, and gave it to General Sheridan, who in turn sent it to Grant.

Keefer also copied an encrypted cable message to Napoleon, dated 3 December, Mexico, and could not decipher it. Hopefully, Keefer wrote, the 373-cable-word message might be published in a French newspaper, and then the American consul or minister could forward a copy to him so he could work out the key in order that he could decrypt future messages between Napoleon and Maximilian. Keefer urged General Grant not to mention the cipher clerk's name in this matter because the telegraph lines were in the control of Southern men, and if they suspected his intentions they would not allow him to come any place where he could hear the instrument "clicking."[49] It is likely Keefer never received the plain text of the encrypted message and therefore could not work out the key; however, this message, from Marshal Bazaine and General Castelnau, was published in 1930 in a biography of General Castelnau.[50] It told of Maximilian's desire to stay in Mexico; in addition, the two French officers wrote that since the evacuation was to be completed in March, it was urgent for the transports to arrive. Would it be possible, they asked, for the French officers and soldiers attached to the Mexican Corps to have the option of returning?

Keefer wrote to Seward directly in early January, telling him the New Orleans newspapers were printing a telegraphic synopsis of the 3 December Bazaine-Castelnau dispatch to Napoleon and requested the secretary to send him a plaintext copy so that he could work out the key to the encrypted intercept he held. He also reported he had intercepted a dispatch from a reporter for *The New York Herald*, sent from New Orleans to the editor, James Bennett. The reporter's dispatch, datelined from Paris, described the fact that the War Cabinet in Vienna had told the Austrian commander of the corvette *Dandelo* at Vera Cruz to remain there until further orders, and also that Napoleon knew this. Keefer emphasized the dispatch never came from Paris at all but originated in New Orleans, and the writer told Bennett to publish it as European news from Paris.

General Sheridan found Keefer's aggressive practices of great value, and he rewarded the young man with a cash prize of $1,600 for managing a secret telegraph line, working out the cipher duplicate messages from Napoleon and the Europeans involving

Maximilian and others in Mexico, and counteracting the machinations of a secret society in New Orleans and in the South. However, despite Sheridan's statement, there is no evidence in the remaining historical records that Keefer successfully decrypted the French dispatches.[51]

Keefer's secret intelligence work continued with a dispatch to Seward on 11 January: he included the text of a forty-nine-word cable message in French, sent in the clear, from Napoleon in Paris to General Castelnau, dated 10 January. The emperor cabled as follows: "Received your despatch of the 9th December. Do not compel the Emperor to abdicate, but do not delay the departure of the troops; bring back all those who will not remain there. Most of the fleet has left."[52] Keefer enclosed the complete cable text, transmitted via the French consul in New Orleans, and suggested that it gave a clue to Napoleon's policy for Mexico.

Keefer's final letter one week later to Seward, who was apparently troubled by Keefer's intercept practices, was an apology. The chastened cipher clerk explained his only motive in sending the previous information was to be of service to the government: "I did not exactly consider myself as playing the part of a spy but on the contrary I considered it my duty as cipher operator . . . to send you copies of the despatches concerning Maximilian."[53] Continuing his letter of justification, Keefer wrote that he realized the secretary of war had removed all restrictions on telegraphic correspondence the previous April; however, Keefer thought the current affairs in Mexico "would warrant me" in telling you of the policy Napoleon intended to pursue towards Maximilian.

Keefer's final request to Seward was not to mention his name regarding this matter since it would harm his prospects as a telegraph operator on the Southern lines. And this melancholy supplication concluded the first peacetime communications intelligence effort. Apparently, Keefer did not realize that "Gentlemen do not read each other's mail."

Earlier State Department monthly bills in 1866 for using the domestic telegraph lines were modest: for example, those received for September that, with an eight percent discount, amounted to $73.79; for October, $76.34.[54] The November telegraph bill amounted to $46.94. And then came the astonishing charges for the 23 November cable to Bigelow – $19,540.50. This cost together with other cables sent in November added up to $24,996.12, an amount equal to the yearly salary of the president of the United States and three times more than that paid the secretary of state.[55] Secretary Seward was unwilling and unable to pay the cable charges.

At the request of William Seward, Cyrus Field, the creative manager of the New York, Newfoundland and London Telegraph Company, met with Seward in Washington to discuss the $25,000 bill.[56] Wilson Hunt accompanied Field. In many ways it was a delicate mission, for the company desperately wanted the government's business, Seward's good will, and the money. Field did not forget that future cable projects might require American governmental support. During the hour-long visit in the secretary's office, Seward complained that whereas he wrote a dispatch of only 780 words in plain text, and had William Hunter, second assistant secretary of the State Department, put the message in code, the charges were for 3,722 words.[57] Field carefully replied that the message came to the telegraph office in code, and it was transmitted exactly as submitted; moreover, he added, Seward would have considered it a "great piece of impertinence on our part if we had asked him" to change the dispatch. Besides, Field added, the company charged him no more than it charged other governments.[58]

Embarrassed and without sufficient funds, Seward asked Field to accept a partial payment of between $5,000 and $6,000, based on the number of words in the original message; if Field approved, the company would eventually be paid in full, and the department would continue using the cable frequently.[59] Seward explained that Congress had not appropriated sufficient funds that would enable him to pay this account. Field then questioned him about the wisdom of using a cipher that had been in use since the formation of the nation. Seward quickly replied that a new economical cipher would replace the old one. In Field's judgment, it was evident Seward had made a great blunder, that when he ordered the dispatch to be put in cipher, he did not realize it would amount to such a large expense. Hunt explained that they were not authorized to accept this $5,00 compromise because his company had already paid the money to the other companies and that at the end of every month, the account was made up. Western Union then took out its money and paid the balance over to the New York, Newfoundland, and London Company, which took out its share. The balance was remitted to London.[60] After a few more minutes of conversation, the secretary finally stated again he would not pay the bill. However, he invited the gentlemen to dine with him.[61]

Somebody leaked the news on the Seward-Field-Hunt private conference to *The New York Herald*, for on 27 December the editor reported inaccurately that the cable company charged $25,000 for the 23 November Seward dispatch and that Seward, not having sufficient funds, paid only $5,000 on it. And then the newsman added with sarcasm: "The United States government must be in a very bad way. All our cable despatches which we have received since the opening of the line were paid for in gold at the other side of the Atlantic, without any reservation or deduction, and we never made any demand for abatement or delay in the payment." The editor concluded, "It is a shame for the United States government not to be able to pay its telegraph bills as promptly as a New York newspaper."

That same day, Hunt and Field hastily composed a telegram of apology to Seward, explaining that upon their return from Washington, they had reported the results of their Seward interview to the directors of the Telegraph Company; however, where and how the *Herald* obtained its information they did not know, and they regretted the editorial very much.[62] An equally prompt reply from Seward acknowledged their note and added that he had no doubt the journal obtained its information from a source unknown to them.[63]

Though a nervous Napoleon had been "scolded" out of Mexico when the final French troops left Vera Cruz on March 11, the diplomacy between Seward and the New York cable company about the unpaid charges totaling $24,935.75 for the three November cipher messages continued to embarrass both parties. However, the State Department continued to use the cable: in December, for messages to Paris, Alexandria, London, and Liverpool with one message in code, and five messages in plain text at a total cost of $743.50. Three messages in January to London and Copenhagen, two in code and one in plain text, totaled $615; only one message, to Nice, for $77.25 was sent in February. Two messages, one in code, one in plain text to London in March, at a cost of $1,157.50, were transmitted.[64] The charges for all these cables were paid in gold by the department in early May when Leonard Whitney presented the bill to Seward in person; however, the bill for the three November code cables remained unpaid. Seward told Whitney that Field and Hunt knew the reasons for his refusal.[65]

Another unique cable dispute involving Seward began on Monday, 25 March 1867, with the transmission of an encrypted 1,833-word (the cable company called them "words"; however, they were cipher characters) cable from the Russian minister, Edouard de Stoeckl, to St. Petersburg. The dispatch began:

t5e51ydzs7x2l2kvzzkgte74z6xoykj8vwz747ng20p5jglgwy3x7zt8e8t2dkg8yfzlk
3ytde69ssp5oyt4krr1lokkftx122g2k5n3etgfnjtrfj1yx6k1zdlgw3pn55

and continued for more than forty-nine lines of encryption. This message is the first encrypted cable ever sent by a foreign minister over State Department lines. It was transmitted through the newly organized State Department telegraph office to Prince Aleksandr Gorchakov, vice chancellor of the Russian Empire, in St. Petersburg at a cost of $9,886.50.[66]

The lengthy cable by the dean of the diplomatic corps in Washington and Seward's friend, contained, encrypted in French, the basic treaty conditions for the purchase of Russian America for $7 million. Stoeckl closed the cable with a firm note of economy and extreme urgency: "I send this telegram at the request of Seward who pays for it and who said to me that he has met with great opposition in the Cabinet because of the sum agreed on and that for the affair to succeed it will be necessary to make haste and to have the treaty confirmed by the Senate which is to sit for two weeks longer. If I receive reply within six days the treaty can be signed and confirmed next week by the Senate."[87]

The Russian government promptly replied to Stoeckl with qualified approval; $200,000 had to be added to the price in order to cover any claims by the Russian-American Company. Seward, anxious to acquire this vast territory, agreed and quickly prepared the necessary documents. Final negotiations for the purchase of Alaska, which Seward considered his greatest achievement as secretary of state, concluded at 4 A.M. on 30 March with the signing at the State Department office. According to one account, Seward, hoping to win over the recalcitrant chairman of the Senate Foreign Relations Committee, Charles Sumner, invited him to the early morning signing ceremony; however, Sumner went to Seward's residence by mistake and missed the function. Nevertheless, Sumner eventually supported the expansionist treaty, and the Senate advised ratification on 9 April by an overwhelming vote.[68]

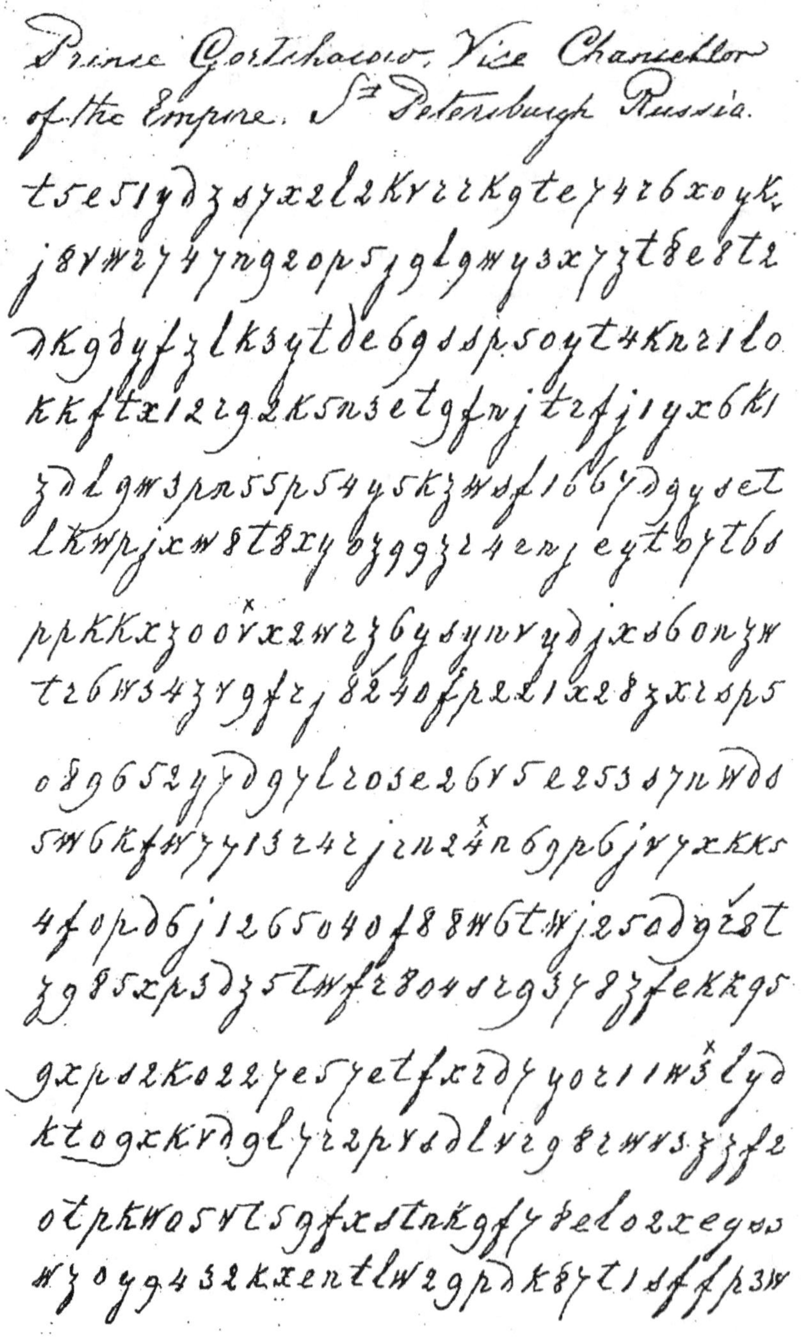

Prince Gortchacow, Vice Chancellor
of the Empire. St Petersburgh Russia.

(enciphered message text, handwritten)

Russian cable regarding Alaska sent from U.S. State Department, March 1867

As noted above, Whitney's visit to Seward on 3 May resulted in a partial payment of cable charges. However, now almost $10,000 for the Russian encrypted cable originally charged to the Russian legation was transferred to the American account at the order of Stoeckl. In addition, two cables from Seward to Adams on 15 and 23 May, sent in the Monroe code, added another $7,300 to the unpaid account, bringing the total to over $42,000. The troublesome account also increased Hunt's and Field's financial anxieties by late May. Hunt telegraphed Seward, stating he and Field were going to Washington and asking if it would be convenient for them to visit the secretary. An adamant and adroit Seward promptly replied he would be delighted to see them socially at any time; however, he would not hold any interview concerning the cable telegrams. He also cabled his minister in France, John A. Dix, and Charles Francis Adams in London to "use the cable no more in cipher or writing. It will not be used here."[69]

A disappointed Hunt, still financially sensitive to Seward's power, quickly replied by letter on 1 June to Seward and recounted the previous tariff schedule and Hunt's understanding that Seward would write to him about reducing the cable charges; however, Hunt again explained, no letter from Seward had arrived. During November, he continued, the State Department dispatches were promptly transmitted but never paid. Instead, the New York Company, which would have kept less than one third of the amount, remitted two thirds of the bill out of its own funds to London for payment. Further construction expenses by the Newfoundland Company for two new landlines in Newfoundland and a contract for a sea cable to be laid from Newfoundland to the French island of St. Pierre, and thence to Sydney, were pressing the company treasury. Hunt concluded cautiously, "Although the company are greatly in want of money, they would not press their claim at this time if it be inconvenient or embarrassing to the Government. But the company have a greater trouble, and one that is exceedingly embarrassing, that is a refusal on the part of the Government, after having used the telegraph, and we having assumed and paid two-thirds for the Government, to acknowledge the debt."[70] Hunt did not mention the bill for the Russian cable.

Always a tough negotiator, Seward sent a two-sentence reply: "I have received and attentively read your letter of the 1st instant. I am, dear sir, Your obedient servant."[71] One week later, Leonard Whitney, cashier for the telegraph company, asked George Baker, the department accounting clerk, if he could collect for the May cable messages and received a prompt "No."[72]

Seward's unhappiness with the cable costs for transmitting dispatches masked by the Monroe code brought into existence the first new State Department code in fifty years. This extremely awkward code, devised for economy, was based upon the letters of the alphabet. The twenty-three words most frequently used in dispatches were assigned one letter of the alphabet. For example, "a" was *the*; "b" was *It*; "c" was *Have*, and so on. "W" was not used for the code (though it was in cipher) because European telegraph operators were not familiar with this letter. The next 624 most frequently used words were encoded by two letters of the alphabet: for example, "ak" for *Those*; "al" for *Who*; and "az" for *such*.

Three letters were used for the remainder of the diplomatic vocabulary, and a fourth letter could be added for plurals, participles, and genitives.

On 19 August 1867, a copy of the new code was sent to John A. Dix, minister to France, and to Cassius Clay, minister to Russia, and to other ministers.[73] For security purposes, Seward asked that the code be used with discretion and also that the minister should have a small box made that could be fastened with a lock, the key to which should be kept by the head of the legation.

This novel code, which delighted the thrifty Seward, was used between August 1867 and 1876 but proved to be a disaster because European and American telegraphers often merged code groups, and dispatches were frequently unread until mailed copies reached the State Department weeks later. Indeed, the first encoded message received at the department from the American minister in Turkey formed a long string of connected letters and remained a conundrum until finally decrypted by an assistant clerk after days of puzzlement. Similar messages came from Paris and one from Vienna; the latter one was never decoded.[74] Seward's battle with the cable company resulted in this supposedly thrifty but flawed encryption system.[75]

A tedious exchange of letters ensued in November 1867, after the New York Company and Hunt informed Seward of its new tariff. The two men corresponded until late 1868, when Seward left office. The telegraph company continued its requests for payment with the new secretary of state, Hamilton Fish. Fish, however, reiterated Seward's positions on the cables.

Finally, on 25 February 1870, the New York, Newfoundland and London Telegraph Company filed a petition in the United States Court of Claims and requested that the government pay $32,240.75 in gold coin for the cable messages from the Department of State to Paris and London. [76]

The "Argument for the Claimant," covering twenty-six pages, submitted on 13 March 1871, to the U.S. Court of Claims for the December term, 1870, reviewed the previous correspondence and depositions taken in the case. Especially notable was Hamilton Fish's agreement that the accounts in the claimant's petition were accurate except for the Russian cable, which the State Department neither authorized nor paid. The claimants agreed with Fish's assertion. The Argument also highlighted the conversations between Hunt and Seward as stated in the depositions before coming to the conclusion that there was no evidence for a special agreement, binding upon the claimant, through which the United States government would have the right to send telegrams over its own and connecting lines at rates lower than the customary charges for sending telegrams by private parties. Thorough in gathering data for the Argument, the lawyers for the claimants also emphasized that the appropriations were adequate for payment of the charges.

Department of State of the U.S.,

To the New York, Newfoundland and London Telegraph Company, Dr.

MESSAGES RECEIVED	FROM WHOM	TO WHOM	DESTINATION	NO. OF WORDS		AMOUNT COIN	DATE OF PAYMENT	AMOUNT PAID, COIN	AMOUNT UNPAID, COIN
1866							**1867**		
Nov. 10 ...	Seward	Bigelow	Paris	23	E	$60 37	May 4	$60 37	
" 24 ...	Seward	Bigelow	Paris	3722	C	19,540 50			$19,540 50
" 29 ...	Seward	Adams	London	280	C	1,400 00			1,400 00
" 30 ...	Seward	Bigelow	Paris	761	C	3,995 25			3,995 25
Dec. 1 ...	Seward	Bigelow	Paris	74	C	388 50	" "	388 50	
" 3 ...	Seward	Hale	Alexandria	36	E	112 50	" "	112 50	
" 3 ...	Seward	Adams	London	16	E	50 00	" "	50 00	
" 11 ...	Seward	Dudley	Liverpool	26	E	65 00	" "	65 00	
" 17 ...	Seward	Dudley	Liverpool	30	E	75 00	" "	75 00	
" 28 ...	Seward	Dix	Paris	19	E	52 50	" "	52 50	
1867									
Jan. 10 ...	Seward	Stevans	London	30	E	75 00	" "	75 00	
" 12 ...	Seward	Yeaman	Copenhagen	63	C	330 00	" "	330 00	
" 29 ...	Seward	Adams	London	42	C	210 00	" "	210 00	
Feb. 5 ...	Seward	Aldis	Nice	30	E	77 25	" "	77 25	
March 7 ...	Seward	Adams	London	215	C	1,075 00	" "	1,075 00	
" 25 ...	Seward	Adams	London	33	E	82 50	" "	82 50	
" 25 ...	....	Gortschacoff* ...	St. Petersburgh ..	1833	E	9,886 50	A'g 22, 1868	9,886 50	
May 15 ...	Seward	Adams*	London	575	C	2,975 00			2,975 00
" 23 ...	Seward	Adams*	London	866	C	4,330 00			4,330 00
" 24 ...	Seward	Adams	London	22	E	55 00	J'ne, '68	52 00	
" 24 ...	Seward	Dix	Paris	22	E	56 75		56 75	
July 16 ...	Seward	Adams	London	13	E	50 00	July 20	50 00	
" 22 ...	Seward	Adams	London	14	E	50 00	Sept. 7	50 00	
" 28 ...	Seward	Adams	London	12	C	100 00	" "	100 00	
" 28 ...	Seward	Adams	London	15	E	50 00	" "	50 00	
Sept. 3 ...	Seward	Yeaman	Copenhagen	26	C	137 50	" 23	137 50	
" 19 ...	Seward	Adams	London	41	E	102 50	" 20	102 50	
" 19 ...	Seward	Hale	Madrid	14	E	53 50	Oct. 14	53 50	
Oct. 5 ...	Seward	Yeaman	Copenhagen	9	C	104 50		104 50	
Total						$45,540 62		$13,299 97	$32,240 75

Transmitted direct by Telegraph from office in Department of State

Cable company memorandum of account with Department of State

Citing more than twenty court cases concerning various aspects of the dispute between the cable company and the State Department, the New York, Newfoundland, and London Telegraph Company lawyers concluded than the claimant should recover the $32,240.75 unless "its rights of recovery is [sic] defeated by the pretended agreement, alleged to have been made between Mr. Seward and the claimant, previous to sending of said dispatches."[77]

The United States's defense regarding the claim specified the government never agreed to pay for the telegraphic service at the published rates. Rather, wrote Thomas H. Talbot, assistant attorney general, it agreed to pay an amount deemed by the secretary of state to be proper compensation. In his deposition, dated 8 August 1870, Seward thought the sum of $5,600 in gold would be a fair, just, and reasonable compensation for the

The case was heard before the Court of Claims in Washington, D.C., on 26 May 1871. In its "Findings of Fact and Conclusions of Law," the court found that the data presented by the claimants were correct, that the secretary of state had paid charges for twenty-three cables (of which seven were encrypted) at regular rates and that he refused to pay five other cable charges, all of them encrypted. Moreover, the company had paid $21,804.90 in gold coin to the connecting lines and was owed this amount plus $10,435.85 for transmission over its own lines, for the total of $32,240.75.

The court decided for the claimant in that amount. The State Department had one victory: payment in gold was not required.[79] Rather, the judgment had to be rendered "in the usual form in dollars and cents, without distinguishing the kind of money in which it shall be paid." Promptly, the New York, Newfoundland and London Telegraph Company's treasurer, Moses Taylor, wrote to the secretary of the treasury requesting that the judgment be immediately paid, or five percent interest be added until paid. He enclosed a certified transcript of the judgment.[80] And finally, on 28 August 1871, almost five years after the Seward-Bigelow cable, the Comptroller's Office paid the full amount in dollars and cents.[81]

(FOUO) Dr. Weber is a professor of history at Marquette University. He completed research for this article while on assignment to the Center for Cryptologic History (September 1991–August 1992) as a scholar-in-residence. He has also served as a scholar-in-residence for the CIA (1987–88). Dr. Weber received an A.B. from St. John's University (1948) and both an M.A. (1950) and a Ph.D. (1956) from the University of Notre Dame. Dr. Weber is the author of *U.S. Diplomatic Codes and Ciphers, 1775–1938* (for which he received the National Intelligence Study Center Scholarly Book Award) and editor of *The Final Memoranda of General Ralph Van Deman.* Dr. Weber currently serves as an associate editor of the *American National Biography* (a new publication that will replace the *Dictionary of American Biography*).

Notes

1. John Bigelow, *Retrospections of An Active Life* (New York: The Baker & Taylor Co., 1909), III, 611. Also cf. Beckles Willson, *American Ambassadors to France 1777–1928* (London: J. Murray, 1928), 287–288. Seward went to extreme lengths to continue the charade, and his numerous dispatches concerning French forces in Mexico continued to flow out of the State Department until March 1867.

2. Bigelow, *Retrospections*, III, 612.

3. Bigelow to Seward, Paris, 3 August 1866, in Record Group 59, General Records of the Department of State, Dispatches from U.S. Ministers to France, Microcopy 34, Roll 62, National Archives. Hereafter cited as RG 59, M34, R62, NA.

4. Ibid. Several years later, Hamilton Fish would cable Robert Schenck, American minister in London, in code and urge him to use code in his dispatches because the telegraph office was leaking information to the newspapers in the United States: cf. Fish to Schenck, Washington, D.C., June 16, 1872, Hamilton Fish Papers, Letter Copy Book, 13 March 1871, to 25 November 1872, Library of Congress, hereafter cited as LC.

5. Bigelow to Seward, 3 August 1866, RG 59, M34, R62, NA.

6. Seward to Bigelow, Washington, D.C., 21 August 1866, Record Group 59, Diplomatic Instructions of the Department of State, Microcopy 77, Roll 58, National Archives. Hereafter cited as RG 59, M77, 58, NA.

7. A determined Bigelow replied to Seward's dispatch by again stating the strong possibility that the cipher at Paris and other legations had been violated by the "treasonable affinities of Mr. [William] Dayton's immediate predecessors . . . ." cf. Bigelow to Seward, Paris, 12 October 1866, RG 59, M34, R62, NA.

8. Bigelow, *Retrospections*, III, 627.

9. Deposition of Wilson G. Hunt, 8 June 1870, RG 123, B307, NA. In a deposition, an onlooker, Mr. Lathers, said at first he thought Seward was being facetious, and the conversation began rather jocularly; it then turned serious as Hunt listened carefully to Seward's criticisms.

10. Petition of the New York, Newfoundland & London Telegraph Co. vs. The United States, filed February 25, 1870, Claim No. 6151, Record Group 59, Microcopy 179, Roll 319, 7, NA. Hereafter cited as the Petition, RG 59, M179, R309, NA. Domestic or landline charges by the Western Union Company were at the regular rate for code and cipher messages; however, cable charges were double: cf. Deposition of Charles Tinker, 16 September 1870, RG 123, B307, NA. Code and cipher messages continued to trouble the telecommunications executives and several systems were tried: for example, fees were based upon five characters per word: cf. James M. Herring and Gerald C. Gross, *Telecommunications: Economics and Regulation* (New York and London: McGraw Hill Book Co., 1936), 138–147.

11. In November 1866, a gold dollar equalled about $1.40 in greenback currency: cf. Wesley Clair Mitchell, *Gold, Prices, And Wages under the Greenback Standard* (Berkeley: The University Press, 1908), 302.

12. Deposition of William Seward, 27 July 1870, RG 123, B307, NA. Seward knew that Hunt, Peter Cooper, and Cyrus Fields, all of New York, were principals in the cable company.

13. Ibid.

14. Deposition of Hunt, ibid.

15. Irwin Unger, *The Greenback Era: A Social and Political History of American Finances, 1865–1879* (Princeton: Princeton University Press, 1964), 16.

16. Deposition of Seward, RG 123, B307, NA.

17. All three depositions, by Hunt, Lathers, and Seward, mention that the secretary would write to the New York telegraph company and offer suggestions for lower rates.

18. Congressional legislation, approved 31 January 1862, authorized the president of the United States to take military possession of the telegraph and railroad lines in the nation. However, in his deposition of 16 September 1870, Charles Tinker, the War Department telegrapher, testified the charges for the government messages sent over the Western Union lines were the same as those for private individuals. The only exceptions were messages sent over the Pacific telegraph lines: these lines were subsidy lines, and the government rate was lower than that fixed for private concerns.

19. Seward's most recent biographer wrote: "Seward was an agitator, a politician, and a statesman, all in one. His irresistible impulse to pose and explain and appear all-wise and all-important earned for him a reputation for insincerity and egotism. A perfectly fair-minded contemporary gave this answer to a question: 'I did not regard Seward as exactly insincere; we generally knew at what hole he would go in, but we never felt quite sure as to where he would come out.' It is a paradox that precisely explains the paradoxical Seward." Cf. John M. Taylor, *William Henry Seward: Lincoln's Right Hand* (New York: Harper-Collins, 1991), 528.

20. *The New York Times*, 13 September 1866.

21. Ibid., 26 October 1866. Less than one year later, this newspaper reported on the financial success of the cable: that two thirds of the entire outlay spent on the cable on 1866 would be returned in revenue from the first year's operation. Moreover, if one were to add the cost of the cable of 1865, the return would be about 30 percent. Thus, rates should be lowered to a moderate scale, wrote the editor, for then the press dispatches could be doubled in length, and "more than doubled in value of their contents." Ibid., 11 July 1867. The source for these cable revenues was not noted by the editor. George Saward, the secretary and general manager for the Atlantic Telegraph Company, stated that the first year's operation of the cable provided a return of only 2 percent on the capital investment: cf. Saward to Hunt, 25 November 1867, in RG 59, M179, R27, NA.

22. The Petition, RG 59, M179, R319, 10–12, NA. As specified in the tariff, all figures in the transmission had to be expressed in words, and charged accordingly. Seward to Bigelow, Washington, D.C., 10 November 1866 in RG 59, M77, R58, NA.

23. Seward to Bigelow, Washington, D.C., 10 November 1866 in RG 59, M77, R58, NA.

24. Deposition of Wilson Hunt, 8 June 1870, RG 123, B307, NA. Also the Petition, RG 59, M179, R319, 15, NA. According to the deposition of Charles Tinker, 16 September 1870, RG 123, B307, NA, the cable company required that the payment in gold for the dispatches should be remitted weekly with a copy of the dispatches. However, in practice, only the dispatches were sent forward, and the Western Union Company billed the particular government office that was specified on the copy of the dispatch.

25. A notable Republican editor called the crisis the "greatest diplomatic difficulty our Government has had for two years," cf. ibid., 21 November 1866.

26. John H. Haswell, "Secret Writing," *The Century Illustrated Monthly Magazine*, 85 (November 1912), 89.

27. On 5 April 1866, *Le Moniteur*, Napoleon's official newspaper, noted that French troops would withdraw on these dates. Cf. Frederic Bancroft, *The Life of William H. Seward* (New York & London: Harper & Brother, 1900), 2:438.

28. John Bigelow to William Seward, Paris, 31 May 1866, as reprinted in *The New York Times*, 7 December 1866. Much of the correspondence between Seward and Bigelow, often confidential, regarding the French status in Mexico is reprinted in this issue of the newspaper. In a 16 May letter to Seward, also reprinted, Bigelow quoted from the 15 May issue of semiofficial newspaper, *La France*, to the effect that the embarkation of Austrian volunteer troops from Mexico had been countermanded, the enlisted men were discharged, and the majority of these troops joined Maximilian's forces. The Mexican crisis, including confidential dispatches, fascinated the press, troubled the Congress, and profoundly worried Seward.

29. *The New York Times*, 30 August 1866. Two weeks earlier, John Hay, charge d'affaires in France, wrote to Seward and reported that the French minister promised "the plan heretofore determined upon by the Emperor's Government will be executed in the way we announced." Cf. John Hay to William Seward, Paris, 17 August 1866, as reprinted in ibid., 7 December 1866. The New York newspaper enthusiastically supported Seward's foreign policies regarding Mexico. Recalling the Monroe Doctrine, the *Times*'s editor wrote: "This country is directly interested in this question and the people will insist that its interests shall be protected. Neither France nor any other European Power can be allowed to gain such a foothold on this continent as the establishment of an empire in Mexico, under her protection, would give them. It would be a perpetual menace to our own security." Ibid., 1 September 1866.

Record Group 59, Confidential Memorandum, Department of State, 17 September 1866 in Administrative Records of the Department of State, Reports of Clerks & Bureau Officers, Entry 311, Volume 4, NA.

31. William Seward to John Bigelow, Washington, D.C., 8 October 1866, as reprinted in *The New York Times*, 7 December 1866.

32. Just a month before, Seward had written to Bigelow that the U.S. "relies with implicit confidence upon the fulfillment of the Emperor's engagement at least to the letter, and it has even expected that, overlooking the letter, it would be fulfilled with an earnestness of spirit which would hasten instead of retard the evacuation of the French forces in Mexico." Seward to Bigelow, Washington, D.C., 8 October 1866 in *The New York Times*, 7 December 1866.

33. John Bigelow to William Seward, Paris, 8 November 1866, in RG 59, M34, R64, NA.

34. Bigelow to Seward, Paris, 8 November 1866, as reprinted in *The New York Times*, 7 December 1866.

35. Glyndon G. Van Deusen, *William Henry Seward* (New York: Oxford University Press, 1967), 494–495.

36. At least one principal European power was using a code similar to the Monroe Code: cf. Haswell, "Secret Writing," *Monthly Magazine* 85 (November 1912), 88. Haswell does not specify the particular nation; however, he probably had reference to France, which was using a code with similar Arabic numerals (2209 613 562 273 15 2214 etc.) and which Charles Keefer, General Sheridan's cipher clerk, intercepted in New Orleans in December 1866: cf. Seward Papers, Microcopy, Roll 98, Library of Congress. Hereafter cited as Seward Papers, R98, LC.

37. *The New York Times*, 24 November 1866, noted the session as an "extraordinary convening of that body" and speculated that the discussions focused on the withdrawal of French troops from Mexico.

38. Deposition of William Seward, 27 July 1870, RG 123, B307, NA. When asked if he had written to Mr. Hunt or the New York Telegraph Company regarding his suggestions for lower cable rates, Seward replied he had not done so, "that it would be inexpedient and unbecoming to make such explanations."

39. Hunt to Seward, New York, 25 November 1866, in RG 59, M179, R246, NA.

40. *New York Herald*, 7 December 1866.

41. John Haswell to John Sherman, Washington, D.C., 20 January 1898. Photocopy in author's possession: the original letter is in the possession of Mrs. Lester Thayer, Albany, New York.

42. General Philip Sheridan and 30,000 troops just north of the Rio Grande River added emphasis to Seward's message: Taylor, *William Henry Seward*, 269.

43. *The New York Herald*, 7 December 1866.

44. The plain text of the encrypted cable from Seward to Bigelow, Washington, 23 November 1866, may be found in RG 59, M77, R58, NA.

45. Bigelow to Seward, Paris, 30 November 1866, Seward Papers, R98, LC. Also cf. Bigelow, *Retrospections*, III, 622–626, for Bigelow's evaluation of the French situation: that delaying the evacuation was merely an "abbreviation rather than a prolongation of her occupation of the Republic of Mexico."

46. Bigelow to Seward, Paris, 3 December 1866, RG 59, M34, R64, NA. This letter is also reprinted in House Executive Documents, 1:1, 39th Congress, Second Session, Serial 1281. Seward honored Bigelow's draft for 9,164 francs, 75 centimes: cf. Seward to Dix, Washington, D.C., 28 December 1866, RG 59, M77, R58, NA. Bigelow's comments on Seward's political maneuvering with Congress regarding Mexico were reprinted in Beckles Willson, *American Ambassadors to France, 1777–1927* (London: J. Murray, 1928), 287–288. Apparently, Seward went to extreme lengths to continue the maneuvers because his numerous dispatches concerning French forces in Mexico continued to reflect heightened anxiety until the actual troop removal was completed in March 1867.

47. William Seward to John Bigelow, Washington, 23 November 1866, in Record Group 84, Instructions to the United States Legation at Paris, Ci.1, NA. The letter book copy of the dispatch may be found in Diplomatic Instructions of the Department of State, 1801–1906, RG 59, M77, R58, NA. At 3:10 p.m. on 25 November 1866, the U.S. military telegraph office in Washington received Hunt's telegram to Seward from New York and reported that the dispatch had been sent to Paris the previous night: RG 59, M34, R64, NA. According to *The New York Herald*, 15 December 1866, Bigelow received the first sheet of the encoded dispatch on Monday morning, 26 November at 7:30, and the last page on Tuesday at 4 a.m.

48. William R. Plum, *The Military Telegraph During the Civil War in the United States* (New York: Arno Press, 1974), 2:357.

49. Keefer to Grant, New Orleans, 17 December 1866, Seward Papers, R98, LC.

50. Georges A.M. Girard, *La Vie et les souvenirs du General Castelnau* (Paris, 1930), 117–118. The actual message is reprinted by E.C. Fishel in his fine article, "A Precursor of Modern Communications Intelligence," *NSA Technical Journal*, 3 (July 1958), 13–14.

51. Philip Sheridan Papers, Microcopy, Roll 2, LC. Sheridan wrote out this message sometime after 1871. He explained he had given this amount of money to Keefer on or about 24 December 1866; he added that the memorandum and reports on Keefer's operations were destroyed in the Chicago fire of 1871. Chicago was the headquarters of the Military Division of Missouri, and when the city burned, the headquarters and all of General Sheridan's records were destroyed. In an attempt to reconstruct the record, Sheridan had two clerks in Washington copying everything relating to his campaigns as filed in the War Department, and these copies constitute a large amount of the Sheridan Papers in the Library of Congress. Cf. George A. Forsyth to General Adam Badeau, Chicago, 21 November 1873, in the NHPRC Search Sheets for U.S. Grant, Library of Congress.

52. Keefer to Seward, New Orleans, 11 January 1867, Seward Papers, R99, LC. General Philip Sheridan, in his book, mistakenly stated the dispatch was received in cipher and translated by the telegraph operator, [Keefer] "who long before had mastered the key of the French cipher." There is no evidence Keefer ever solved the French cipher. Philip H. Sheridan, *Personal Memoirs of P.H. Sheridan* (New York: Charles C. Webster & Co., 1888), 2:226. Sheridan also sent a copy of Napoleon's dispatch to General Ulysses S. Grant from New Orleans, 12 January 1867, and wrote that the dispatch was genuine. Ulysses S. Grant Papers, Microcopy, Roll 24, LC. Sheridan's copy is in his Papers, R47, LC.

53. Keefer to Seward, New Orleans, 17 January 1867, ibid. Copies of Seward's replies to Keefer have not been located in the Seward Papers nor in the State Department files in the National Archives.

54. Leonard Whitney to George Baker, Washington, D.C., 20 November 1866. RG 59, Records of the Bureau of Account: Miscellaneous Letters Received, Entry 212, NA.

55. Leonard Whitney to George Baker, Washington, D.C., 17 December 1866, ibid. Whitney, cashier for the Western Union Telegraph Company, seemed unconcerned about the huge increase in the monthly bill, for he wrote "Please indicate what corrections, if any, are to be made in bills and return to me and I will send them to you recptd." He would soon learn there was a problem: Baker, the disbursing clerk of the State Department, wrote to him, enclosed money for the December telegraph bill and added "No arrangement has yet been made with the Atlantic Telegraph Co." Cf. Baker to Whitney, 18 January 1867, RG 59, Records of the Bureau of Account: Miscellaneous Letters Sent, Entry 202, NA. John H. Haswell, "Secret Writing," in *The Century Illustrated Monthly Magazine*, 85 (November 1912), 89. He wrote that the cost of the cable exceeded $23,000. Cf. Fletcher Pratt in *Secret and Urgent: The Story of Codes and Ciphers* (Indianapolis and New York: Bobbs-Merrill, 1939), 191-192, and Clifford Hicks in "Tales from the Black Chambers," *American Heritage*, 24 (April 1973), 58: both authors state $23,000 as the cost. E. Wilder Spaulding, *Ambassadors Ordinary and Extraordinary* (Washington D.C.: Public Affairs, 1961), 72, notes the cost at $13,000; and Bigelow in *Retrospections*, 611, wrote that the State Department was charged something over $13,000.

56. Fields received a letter from Baker, which included Seward's request to come to Washington for a discussion of the cable issue: cf. Fields to Seward, New York City, 12 December 1866, Seward Papers, R98, LC. The Hunt Deposition also notes that he and Field went to Washington at Seward's request: Deposition of Wilson G. Hunt, RG 123, B307, NA.

57. Hunter, from Rhode Island, began his service in the State Department in 1829, served under twenty-one different secretaries of state and twelve presidents, and would clerk for more than fifty-five years. Cf. Page proof of Whitelaw Reid's column on Hunter for *The New York Daily Tribune*, which Reid sent Hamilton Fish, 20 May 1879, in the Hamilton Fish Papers, Container 123, LC.

58. Deposition of Cyrus Fields, 23 August 1870, RG 123, B307, NA.

59. Deposition of Wilson G. Hunt, 8 June 1870, ibid. Seward's biographer, Glyndon Van Deusen, found a Machiavellian streak in him, "a love for obfuscating his adversaries by ambiguities that on occasion bewildered even his friends," cf. *Seward*, 565.

60. Within the next year or so, the State Department owed a total of $32,240.75, and of that amount, Western Union received $933.20; the Anglo-American and other European companies, $20,871.70; and finally, the amount which the New York Newfoundland and London Company should have received was $10.435.85. Cf. Deposition of Henry H. Ward, 5 October 1870. RG 123, B306. NA.

61. Ibid.

62. Hunt and Field to Seward, New York, 27 December 1866, as reprinted in the Petition, RG 59, M179, R319, 34, NA.

63. Seward to Field and Hunt, Washington, 29 December 1866, Seward Papers, R98, LC.

64. The Petition, RG 59, M179, R319, 15, NA.

65. Deposition of Leonard Whitney, 12 October 1870, RG 123, B306, NA.

66. Stoeckl to Gorchakov, Washington, D.C., 25 March 1867, RG 59, Telegrams Sent by the Department of State, 1867–69, Entry 309, National Archives. Hereafter cited as RG 59, E209, NA. Stoeckl would use the State Department telegraph office for two more telegrams (the State Department was charged $49.97) on 22 May and 25 May 1867, when he telegraphed the Russian consul, Martin Klinkowstrvern, in San Francisco and told him the Alaskan Treaty had been ratified by the emperor and thus American ships and merchandise could be landed free in the new northwest American possessions. He also cabled Gorchakov again on 20 June 1867, notifying him ratifications had been exchanged. This time, $69 in gold was paid the same day: cf. RG 59, E209, NA.

67. Stoeckl to Gorchakov, Washington, D. C., 25 March 1867, ibid.

68. Taylor, *Seward*, 278. According to another account, Sumner went to Seward's house, where he learned from Stoeckl and Frederick Seward that a treaty was being prepared; Stoeckl then went to the State Department to meet with Secretary Seward and complete the treaty; however, Sumner went to his own home at 322 I Street. Cf. Van Deusen, *Seward*, 541. Apparently, Seward added the $200,000 to the purchase price on his own authority: cf. Ronald J. Jensen, *The Alaska Purchase and Russian-American Relations* (Seattle and London: University of Washington Press, 1975), 77.

69. Hunt to Seward, the Petition, RG 59, M179, R319, NA. Also Seward to Dix, Washington, D.C., 24 May 1867 in RG 59, M77, R58, NA. Seward to Dix and Adams, 24 May 1867 in RG 59, E209, NA. The cable charges of $111.75 in gold were paid two weeks later, and subsequent cables were also paid within a few days after transmission.

70. Hunt to Seward, New York, 1 June 1867, as reprinted in the Petition, RG 59, M319, R319, 35–37, NA.

71. Seward to Hunt, Washington, D.C., 11 June 1867, in ibid., 38.

72. Whitney to Baker, Washington, D.C. 19 June 1867, RG 59, E209, NA.

73. Seward to Dix. Washington.D.C.. 19 August 1867; same date for dispatch to Clay. RG59. M77. R58. NA.

74. John Haswell to Hamilton Fish, Washington, D.C., 8 July 1873, Hamilton Fish Papers, R95, LC.

75. State Department Telegrams, 1867–1869, in RG 59, E209, NA reflect the complications posed by this code. Also many other dispatches to and from U.S. ministers during these years contain other examples of this defective code design.

76. The Petition, RG59, M179, R319, 56, NA.

77. "Argument for the Claimant," RG 123, B306, 26, NA.

78. "Brief in Defense" filed in the Court of Claims of the United States, 3 May 1871, RG 123, B306, NA. Also, Seward Deposition, 8 August 1870 in ibid.

79. Had payment in gold been stipulated, the cost to the government would have been $35,787 in greenback currency: cf. Mitchell, *Gold*, 316.

80. Taylor to George Boutwell, New York, N.Y., 6 June 1871, Record Group 217, Accounting Office of the Treasury Department, Office of the First Auditor, Misc. Treasury Account 180406, NA.

81. No. 180406, Comptroller's Office, 28 August 1871, ibid.

www.ingramcontent.com/pod-product-compliance
Lightning Source LLC
Chambersburg PA
CBHW081143280526
45787CB00007B/3204